BATTLE ROAD

BATTLE

Birthplace of the American Revolution

ROAD

by MAURICE R. CULLEN, Jr.   drawings by HOWARD L. RICH

THE CHATHAM PRESS, INC.

Old Greenwich, Connecticut

Distributed by
THE VIKING PRESS, INC.

Contents

American Participants 6

British Participants 7

Introduction 9

Battle Road 11

The Capture of Paul Revere 16

Josiah Nelson House 16

The Hartwell Houses 17

Meriam's Corner 18

Concord 18

MAPS OF THE BATTLE ROAD 23

The North Bridge 28

The Bloody Angle 37

Retreat to Charlestown 44

American Participants

HANNAH ADAMS: of Menotomy; mother of a newborn baby forced from her home by British soldiers.

SAMUEL ADAMS and JOHN HANCOCK: patriot leaders visiting the home of the Reverend Jonas Clark on the night of April 18–19.

HANNAH BARNS: of Concord; refused to permit British troops to search her quarters in Ephraim Jones's tavern.

AMOS BARRETT: Concord minuteman who witnessed many of the events of April 19.

COLONEL JAMES BARRETT: commanding officer of the Concord area militia.

MAJOR JOHN BUTTRICK: second in command of Concord's forces.

THE REVEREND JONAS CLARK: Lexington minister and leading patriot.

BENJAMIN and RACHEL COOPER: escaped to the safety of their cellar when British troops entered their tavern in Menotomy.

CAPTAIN ISAAC DAVIS: of Acton; killed at North Bridge.

WILLIAM DAWES: carried word of the British march from Boston to Lexington over a route different from that taken by Paul Revere.

THE REVEREND WILLIAM EMERSON: Concord minister and eyewitness to events of April 19th in Concord.

THE REVEREND EBENEZER FOSTER: member of the Reading company who saw action at Meriam's Corner during the return march of the British.

JONATHAN HARRINGTON: Lexington militiaman killed on the Battle Green.

EPHRAIM HARTWELL: alerted of the British march by Dr. Prescott, he attempted to get word to the commander of Lincoln's minutemen.

MARY HARTWELL: daughter-in-law of Ephraim, she learned of the British march from his frightened servant and carried the word to Captain William Smith of the Lincoln Minute Company. The following morning she witnessed the fine precision of the regulars as they marched by her house.

SAMUEL HARTWELL: Mary's husband, and member of the Lincoln minutemen.

JAMES HAYWARD: an Acton minuteman killed at the well on the Fiske property.

GENERAL WILLIAM HEATH: first general to take command of American troops in the field, he tried to form the minute and militia companies into an effective fighting force on April 19th.

ABNER HOSMER: Acton minuteman killed at North Bridge.

LIEUTENANT JOSEPH HOSMER: took part in the fight at North Bridge.

ELISHA JONES: a resident of Concord, he lived in the famed "Bullet-Hole House" across the street from North Bridge; witnessed the activities around North Bridge.

EPHRAIM JONES: Concord innkeeper and jailer.

JOSIAH NELSON: a resident of Lincoln, he carried the alarm to Bedford during the night of April 18–19.

CAPTAIN JOHN PARKER: commanding officer of the Lexington militia.

DR. SAMUEL PRESCOTT: Concord resident who joined Revere and

Dawes in Lexington; escaped capture and carried the alarm to Ephraim Hartwell, of Lincoln, and then to patriots in Concord.

PAUL REVERE: an American patriot and courier who rode to Lexington to warn Samuel Adams and John Hancock that the British were on the way.

LIEUTENANT COLONEL JOHN ROBINSON: Acton resident who led the American march on North Bridge with Major Buttrick.

JASON RUSSELL: resident of Menotomy killed in his front yard by British troops.

WILLIAM THORNING: a Lincoln minuteman who killed two British soldiers by firing from behind a boulder in Josiah Nelson's pasture.

AMMI WHITE: a Concord minuteman who killed a wounded British soldier at North Bridge.

SAMUEL WHITNEY: a leading Concord patriot and minuteman who lived in what is now called "The Wayside."

JASON WINSHIP and JABEZ WYMAN: brothers-in-law killed by the British in the Cooper Tavern, Menotomy.

SIMON WINSHIP: a citizen of Lexington seized by British soldiers during the night of April 18–19 and forced to march with them; witnessed the fight on Lexington Green on the morning of the 19th.

British Participants

LIEUTENANT JOHN BARKER: King's Own Regiment; witnessed most of the activity of April 18–19.

ENSIGN HENRY DE BERNIERE: 10th Infantry; an eyewitness.

CAPTAIN W. G. EVELYN: King's Own Regiment; marched to Lexington with Percy's relief force on April 19th; witnessed the fighting on the return march.

CAPTAIN WALTER LAURIE: 43rd Infantry; in command of the three companies at North Bridge.

ENSIGN JEREMY LISTER: 10th Infantry; witnessed the actions of April 18–19.

LIEUTENANT FREDERICK MACKENZIE: Royal Welch Fusiliers; marched to Lexington with Percy's relief force; witnessed much of the action on the trek to Charlestown.

CAPTAIN LAWRENCE PARSONS: 10th Infantry; officer in command of the troops sent to North Bridge and to Barrett's farm.

BRIGADIER GENERAL HUGH, EARL PERCY: commanding officer of the force sent to relieve Colonel Smith's troops; Percy assumed overall command during the retreat to Charlestown.

MAJOR JOHN PITCAIRN: Royal Marines; second in command to Colonel Smith.

LIEUTENANT COLONEL FRANCIS SMITH: commanding officer of the 700-man military force that marched to Lexington and Concord on the night of April 18–19.

WHEN THE BRITISH ARMY MARCHED TO LEXINGTON AND CONCORD ON THE night of April 19, 1775, there was no talk on either side of an American Army for no such army existed. The various towns had long supported their own militia units in which all able-bodied men were required to serve. The primary function of the militia was to defend a town or towns against Indian attack or to meet other threats to colonial security.

As conditions became more critical between the colonists and England, special volunteers from the militia were trained to go into action at a "minute's notice," and were, appropriately, called *minutemen*. When word of the British march to Concord reached the towns and villages of Middlesex County—and beyond—the militia and minute companies responded. They fought as separate, loosely organized units in spite of the efforts of General William Heath and Dr. Joseph Warren to mold them into an "army" on April 19th. Had they been more properly organized, had they concentrated their fire along The Battle Road that day, British losses might have been considerably higher than they were.

The Old Burial Ground, Concord

THE WINDING STRETCH OF COUNTRY ROAD EXTENDING FROM LEXINGTON, Massachusetts, to neighboring Concord was touched by history on April 19, 1775. The British Army scuffed the dust from its surface that day, marching to fife and drum through thick woods and sprawling pastureland past the houses and outbuildings of a determined breed of Americans who stood up to British might in the first fire of the American Revolution. It became known as The Battle Road and it still stands. Much of it lies beneath the smooth macadam of Route 2A and what is now Massachusetts Avenue. But in some places the road appears today as it was 200 years ago when critical events were recorded amid the neat stone walls, the old houses, the boulder-strewn fields. The Battle Road is a shrine to American courage.

By mid-April, 1775, conditions between the American colonists and royal officials in Massachusetts had deteriorated to the point where armed conflict was a painful possibility. A long list of tax laws, in addition to certain stormy events brought on when the British tried to force unpopular legislation on the colonists, had widened the rift brought on ten years earlier by passage of the Stamp Act. Samuel Adams, John Hancock, and other radical Whigs, urged Massachusetts patriots to resist further encroachments. In that pursuit, a large quantity of military provisions had been collected at Concord. General Thomas Gage, Royal Governor of the Colony, became aware of the buildup; and, after receiving authority from England, ordered a military force of some 700 men under Lieutenant Colonel Francis Smith to march from Boston to Concord 17 miles away to seize and destroy the provincial supplies. Gage's order was carried out on the night of April 18, 1775.

The statue of Captain John Parker, Lexington Green

Two dedicated patriots, Paul Revere and William Dawes, were selected to ride out along two separate routes to warn Adams and Hancock who were then conferring with fellow Whigs in Lexington. Enroute, Revere "alarmed almost every house" until he entered the town.

In the center of Lexington stands the statue of a town militiaman, its back to the triangular Green which served as the first battleground of the American Revolution. Captain John Parker commanded the Lexington company that fateful night. At the Buckman Tavern near the east side of the Green, he gathered his men to determine what action they should take in the face of the British march. Revere had done his work with dispatch, alerting militia commanders along the way and rousing Adams and Hancock who were staying at the home of the Reverend Jonas Clarke (now the Hancock-Clarke house) about a quarter of a mile from the Common. They were joined later by Dawes who had taken the longer route. Word of the British expedition circulated throughout the town, and Parker readied his men.

". . . The militia of this town were alarmed," the Reverend Clarke noted, "and ordered to meet on the usual place of parade; not with any design of commencing hostilities upon the king's troops, but to consult what might be done for our own and the people's safety. . . ."

At dawn of the 19th, Major John Pitcairn, of the Royal Marines, led six companies of regulars into Lexington. The sun was up, and he could make out Captain Parker and his small band of militia poised at the ready, muskets in hand. Townspeople were there as well, standing about the place in shadowy clots and at first making Pitcairn believe the provincial force to be larger and more formidable than it actually was. Earlier Pitcairn had halted the column a short distance from the town and had given the order to his troops to load their weapons.

John Parker had issued orders to his men as well; they were to stand fast and not fire unless fired upon. The Reverend Clarke put the number of town militia on the Green at about "50 or 60, or possibly more," with others "coming towards it." Then the British marched towards the "east end of said meeting-house, in sight of our militia . . . who were about 12 or 13 rods distant."

At this point, Pitcairn instructed his men to move in among the provincials and disarm them, nothing more. When the regulars neared the colonials, Pitcairn called out to them, as one witness recalled, "Lay down your arms, you damned rebels, and disperse!"

Recognizing that his force was outnumbered and in danger, Parker ordered his militia to break ranks and disperse. Most of them began moving towards the edges of the Green, but they pointedly ignored Pitcairn's order to lay down their arms.

Lined up on the rim of the Common, the infantry proceeded to advance on the American line. Then suddenly their huzzahs and shouts ignited the early quiet and they charged. Some witnesses later testified that Pitcairn rode before his troops shouting at the Americans: "Lay down your arms—damn you—why don't you lay down your arms?" Then a shot rang out—who fired it or from which side it came is still contested. But Simon Winship, a citizen of Lexington who had been seized by the redcoats on the road during the night and forced to march with them, testified that at that moment he saw a British officer "flour-

A Paul Revere lantern

ishing his sword, and with a loud voice" give the word "*fire!*" which was followed by a volley from the redcoats. The infantry swarmed over the triangle then, firing into the Americans, slashing with their bayonets, an armed mob completely out of control. Horrified at what was happening, Pitcairn swung his horse around and rode in among them, calling repeatedly to them to stop firing. The soldiers ignored him.

Slain and injured men were sprawled over the Green. Mortally wounded, Jonathan Harrington crawled from the battleground to his home which still stands at the northwest corner of the Lexington Common. There he died at his wife's feet.

Some Americans returned fire but their scattered bursts did little beyond adding to the smoke. Then Colonel Smith's main force swept into the Common as well, clearing it and the surrounding fields and roads of provincials. That done, the gunfire fell off and the melee was over. After filling their cartridge boxes and loudly saluting their victory, the British columns re-formed and marched down the Concord Road, leaving Lexington to mourn eight dead sons (now entombed beneath the monument on the Common). Ten others were wounded.

By now the sun was full and bright. The air had an early spring snap to it, and trees were "leafing out." Here the terrain differed from the flat open fields to the east. On the Concord side of Lexington the vast farm and pasturelands were broken by ridges and small valleys; the road dipped and rose with the contours of the land, ominous signs for soldiers in a hostile country. The towns had been alerted; the redcoats were a long way from home.

The Buckman Tavern

The Capture of Paul Revere

AFTER ALARMING THE PEOPLE OF LEXINGTON, PAUL REVERE AND WILLIAM Dawes moved on to carry the word to Concord. Dr. Samuel Prescott, a young patriot, joined the two as they set out. A short while later they rode into a patrol of British officers searching for provincial couriers such as themselves. Revere was arrested and detained while Dawes and Prescott escaped, the latter by leaping his horse over a stone wall and riding away. (The place of Revere's capture is marked with a stone monument on The Battle Road west of the Josiah Nelson house site.)

Josiah Nelson House

THE OFFICERS THEN TURNED ABOUT AND STARTED BACK TO LEXINGTON. According to a story told by the family in later years, Josiah Nelson's wife, Mary, heard the clatter of horses outside her home and mistook the redcoat riders for neighboring farmers on their way to early market. Aware that the British were out in force, she urged her husband to inquire if the riders had word of redcoat activity. Josiah went outside and hailed the officers whose scarlet uniforms were concealed beneath black capes. "Have you heard anything about when the regulars are coming out?" he asked.

One of the officers reportedly drew his sword. "We will let you know when they are coming out!" he bellowed, bringing the sword blade down on Nelson's head. It left a bloody gash at the crown.

After being held captive for a short time, Nelson was advised to go home with a warning: "If you give any alarm or light a light, we will burn your house down over your head."

Once at home, Josiah had his wife treat the head wound; then he saddled his horse and rode off to warn the minutemen of Bedford then gathering at the Fitch Tavern.

Revere was released on foot in Lexington while the British officers proceeded to join the main column of regulars on the road from Boston.

The Nelson house was destroyed by fire in 1908. The site can be found in a boulder-strewn field on the north side of The Battle Road as it curves above Route 2A beyond the Jacob Whittemore house.

AFTER ESCAPING FROM THE BRITISH, DR. PRESCOTT, WHO KNEW THE COUNTRY, rode northward through swamps, woods, and fields to the Hartwell Tavern where he roused 66-year-old Ephraim Hartwell and told him of the British march. (Ephraim owned and lived in the Hartwell Tavern which still stands on The Battle Road a short distance to the west of Samuel Hartwell's house.) According to stories passed down by the family, Ephraim quickly directed his slave girl to alert Captain William Smith of the Lincoln minutemen, who lived almost a half mile down the road to the east. The woman started out but panicked in the darkness and ran to the nearby home of Ephraim's son Samuel, a sergeant in the Lincoln company. Samuel's wife, Mary, revealed in later years that she succeeded in calming the frightened girl and drew the story from her. Then, placing her infant child in the slave's arms, she went off to warn Captain Smith herself, while her husband prepared to join his company.

The following morning when Mary Hartwell heard the British approaching from Lexington, she went to her front door. Down the road to the east she recognized the long red line—700 soldiers in white leggings and scarlet coats, the high pointed hats of the grenadiers bobbing as they marched. "The army of the King marched up in fine order," she later recalled, "and their bayonets glistened in the sunlight like a field of waving grain. If it hadn't been for the purpose they came for, I should say it was the handsomest sight I ever saw in my life." After that, Mary Hartwell collected her children and hurried to the safety of her father's home near Lincoln Center.

Meriam's Corner

THE BRITISH COLUMN MOVED ON PAST THE HARTWELL HOUSES TO A POINT where The Battle Road juts sharply to the south, then to the west again and past the homes of Job and Samuel Brooks. At Meriam's Corner (named for the Meriam family whose house still stands at the juncture of Route 2A and the Bedford Road), a hilly ridge reaches up to command the road on its northern side. In plain view of the redcoats, armed minutemen and militia watched silently from the heights as the regulars shuffled along. Colonel Smith, aware of his exposed position, ordered his light infantry to leave the road and sweep the ridge clear of provincials while the grenadiers went on ahead. Slowly, deliberately, careful to stay beyond the grasp of the infantry, the Americans withdrew towards Concord Center.

Concord

HOURS BEFORE, DR. PRESCOTT HAD CARRIED THE ALARM TO CONCORD AND THE people were already tending to their duties. According to the Reverend William Emerson, who lived in the Old Manse alongside Concord's North Bridge, "We were alarmed by the ringing of the bell" between one and two o'clock in

Meriam's Corner

the morning. (The Reverend Emerson, grandfather of Ralph Waldo Emerson, witnessed much of the action in Concord that day.)

Another who was moved to action by the alarm was Samuel Whitney, a prominent patriot and muster master of the Concord minutemen. (Whitney lived in a Battle Road house to the west of Meriam's Corner which, in later years, was to become a literary shrine. Named "The Wayside," by Nathaniel Hawthorne when he lived there, the Alcotts and Margaret Sidney also resided in the house.) Whitney, a member of the Committee of Public Safety, had hidden seven tons of gunpowder and firearms in his barn during the arms build-up preceding the British march to Concord.

About 150 of the town's militia and minutemen gathered, held a council of war and decided "to go out and meet the British." They strode off down the road to meet the 700 redcoats headed in their direction. A short while later they spotted the British column; and when the distance closed to 100 rods, the Americans executed a sharp about-face and started back to town in front of the advancing regulars. "We were ordered to the about face," Corporal Amos Barrett recalled, "and marched before them with our drums and fifes going and also the British. We had grand music."

Back in town, the Americans found the "Alarm Company," a militia unit comprised of older men, lodged on a hill atop the old Burial Ground across the street from the meeting house and the Wright Tavern. At about 7:00 A.M., as the British pressed into the center of Concord, the provincial force slowly withdrew to another hill behind the town overlooking the home of Elisha Jones on present-day Monument Street. Then they moved again, across the Concord

Major John Buttrick's house

The long sword of
Colonel James Barrett

River and north about a mile to Punkatasset Hill overlooking North Bridge. (Above the bridge stands Major John Buttrick's fine house on Liberty Street across from the Park Visitor Center.)

Beyond the bridge two miles to the west on what is now Barrett's Mill Road is the home of James Barrett, colonel of the militia regiment based in the Concord area. His farm was a target of the British for, according to Smith's intelligence, it was a major collecting point for provincial supplies. In later years, his family revealed that balls, flints, and cartridges were packed in barrels and covered with feathers and then were concealed in the attic.

After scanning the town from the burial ground hill, Colonel Smith and Major Pitcairn set up headquarters in the Wright Tavern across the street. The grenadiers were ordered to search the town for military stores and to destroy what they found. Smith then dispatched one company of light infantry to stand guard at South Bridge, which did not seem to be a critical point, and sent a total of seven companies to North Bridge where trouble could be expected. The second contingent he placed under the command of Captain Lawrence Parsons of the 10th Regiment.

The grenadiers moved about the town at will. Having strict orders not to molest the citizens or to trifle with private property, they were almost gentle in their efforts to uncover the provisions, a posture which enabled the patriots to keep most of the supplies, that had not been moved, out of British hands. Ephraim Jones, innkeeper and town jailer, had concealed three 24-pound cannons in his jailyard and hidden a chest belonging to the provincial treasurer in his inn. (Both buildings were located on what is now Main Street just off The

(Continued on page 27)

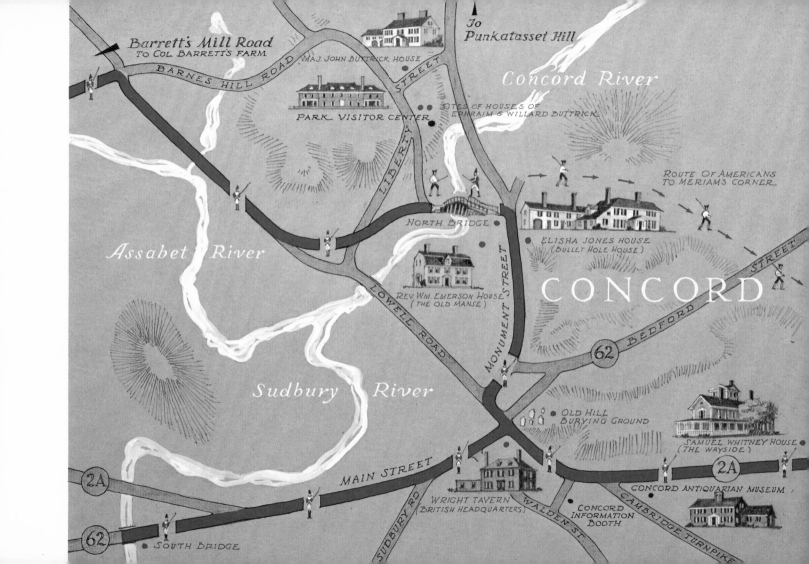

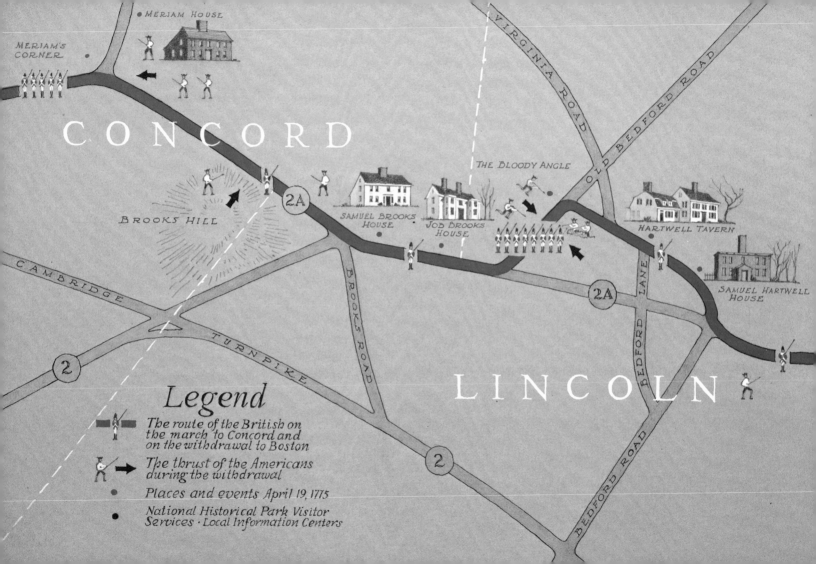

MERIAM HOUSE

MERIAM'S CORNER

CONCORD

VIRGINIA ROAD

OLD BEDFORD ROAD

2A

BROOKS HILL

THE BLOODY ANGLE

SAMUEL BROOKS HOUSE

JOB BROOKS HOUSE

HARTWELL TAVERN

SAMUEL HARTWELL HOUSE

CAMBRIDGE

BROOKS ROAD

2A

BEDFORD LANE

TURNPIKE

2

LINCOLN

Legend

The route of the British on the march to Concord and on the withdrawal to Boston

The thrust of the Americans during the withdrawal

Places and events April 19, 1775

National Historical Park Visitor Services · Local Information Centers

2

BEDFORD ROAD

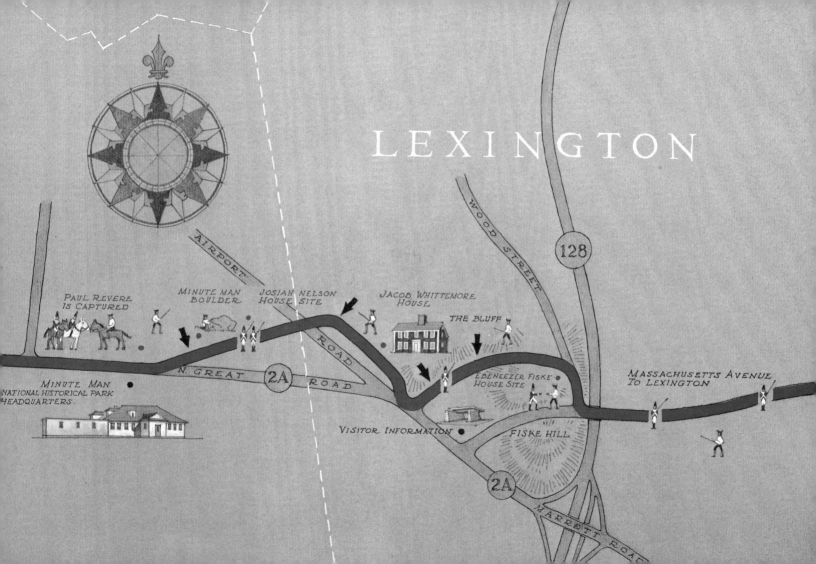

LEXINGTON

PAUL REVERE
IS CAPTURED

MINUTE MAN
BOULDER

JOSIAH NELSON
HOUSE SITE

JACOB WHITTEMORE
HOUSE

THE BLUFF

AIRPORT

ROAD

WOOD STREET

128

MINUTE MAN
NATIONAL HISTORICAL PARK
HEADQUARTERS.

N. GREAT

2A

ROAD

EBENEEZER FISKE
HOUSE SITE

MASSACHUSETTS AVENUE
TO LEXINGTON

VISITOR INFORMATION

FISKE HILL

2A

MARRETT ROAD

4
225

BEDFORD STREET

HANCOCK STREET

● HANCOCK-CLARKE HOUSE

JONATHAN HARRINGTON HOUSE

LEXINGTON GREEN

● BUCKMAN TAVERN

● LEXINGTON INFORMATION CENTER

OLD BELFRY

◄ *Massachusetts Avenue to Concord*

CLARKE STREET

WALTHAM STREET

WOBURN STREET

LOCATION OF BRITISH FIELD
PIECES COVERING THE WITHDRAWAL

LEXINGTON

MUNROE TAVERN
PERCY'S HEADQUARTERS

*Massachusetts Avenue
to Arlington (Menotomy)
& Boston*

2A

Battle Road.) In an effort to protect the items, Jones bolted all the doors and refused to let the soldiers enter either building. But Major Pitcairn arrived to assess matters and ordered that a door be broken down at the jail, a place which was clearly not private property. He then demanded that Jones reveal where the cannons were hidden. With Pitcairn's pistol under his nose, the innkeeper-jailer finally but reluctantly gave in. But not so with the treasurer's chest; the inn was private property. When the grenadiers got to the apartment where the chest had been placed, a young woman named Hannah Barns blocked the doorway, insisting that the place and everything in it were hers. The redcoats shrugged and departed.

With all their efforts, the British found only a small quantity of the provisions; most had long before been moved to other places. What Smith's grenadiers did manage to find and destroy was hardly enough to dampen provincial resolve. According to the Reverend Emerson, the soldiers "set fire to several carriages for the artillery, destroyed 60 barrels of flour, rifled several houses, took possession of the town-house, destroyed 500 lb. of balls . . . ," along with chopping down a liberty pole. They threw some of the cannon balls into the local mill pond only to have the townspeople retrieve them later.

AT NORTH BRIDGE, CAPTAIN PARSONS FOUND HIMSELF COMMANDING A SIZABLE body of troops without being at all certain what to do with them. To begin with, armed minutemen and militia stood on Punkatasset Hill watching the bridge. In the face of that, Parsons had orders to secure the bridge, thus preventing the provincials from re-entering the town, and, in addition, to march

The North Bridge

to Colonel Barrett's farm in search of the hidden stores. So the Captain had to devise a scheme for accomplishing both missions while facing formidable odds. Finally he decided to place his entire force on the west side of the bridge—their backs to the river—and to leave one company to defend it. Captain Walter Laurie was left in command. Satisfied that it was the proper thing to do, Parsons marched off towards Barrett's house two miles away, dropping off two more companies on a range of hills about a quarter of a mile from the bridge (where the Park Visitor Center now stands). Meanwhile, Colonel Barrett raced back to his farm to be certain that the stores had been properly cared for.

The lower hills blocked the Americans' view of the road taken by Parsons. Now reinforced by new militia and minute units from nearby towns, and unclear as to what was happening in the vicinity of the bridge, the provincials decided to move down from Punkatasset for a closer look. As they did so, the two companies of regulars evacuated their position on the lower hills and rejoined Captain Laurie's company at the bridge while the provincials occupied their former positions.

Throughout Colonel Barrett's absence, Major John Buttrick, of Concord, whose home still stands nearby, took an active role in directing the American force. Signs of smoke rising from Concord's town square finally stirred his men. The smoke came from the burning of the few stores the British had managed to collect thus far, but the provincials had no way of knowing that. With rumors of British treachery at Lexington stark in their minds, they were certain that Smith was putting the town to the torch. Their families were there, their property and life's possessions! "Will you let them burn the town down?"

The North Bridge

Colonel Barrett's farm

Lieutenant Joseph Hosmer shouted in anguish. After a hurried conference, the Americans agreed to march into the town and defend it. Mounting his horse, Colonel Barrett, who had returned from his farm, ordered his men to load weapons but not to fire unless fired upon. The provincials formed up in columns of twos and started down the hill.

Captain Laurie, who had sent a messenger to Colonel Smith asking for reinforcements, then ordered the three companies to fall back over the bridge. In the process, several redcoats paused to tear up planks to prevent the Americans from crossing.

Corporal Amos Barrett, marching with the third company of minutemen, carefully noted: "Major Buttrick said if we were all of his mind he would drive them away from the Bridge. They should not tear that up." Buttrick even shouted down at the redcoats demanding that they cease their efforts to destroy the bridge.

In any case, Laurie's men had too little time to tear up more than a few planks or to organize a workable defense. Meanwhile, Captain Parsons and the four companies at Barrett's farm were ignorant of developments and were now isolated behind the provincials, a fact that did not deter some of Laurie's people from trying to render the bridge impassable. That effort was abandoned with the approach of the provincials, and Laurie's troops, packed together on the east side now, made hasty preparations to defend themselves.

The British then fired several scattered warning shots which sent musket balls plopping into the river. When the Americans failed to take heed, a single shot rang out followed almost immediately by a full volley.

The Americans, led by Major Buttrick and Lieutenant Colonel John Robinson, of Westford, and followed by Captain Isaac Davis, of Acton, and Abner Hosmer, an Acton fifer, began closing when the volley exploded from the east side of the bridge. Davis and Hosmer fell dead. A few others suffered wounds. At that point Major Buttrick uttered one of the more colorful orders of the day: "Fire, fellow-soldiers, for God's sake fire!" A fusillade of balls raced through the air and into the redcoats. Corporal Barrett said of the ensuing violence: "The balls whistled well. We were then all ordered to fire that could and not kill our own men."

After other scattered exchanges, the British turned and bolted down the road towards the Square, one of their number killed outright, and eleven wounded, two mortally. Half the officers were among the wounded. Beyond the Elisha Jones house, situated across Monument Street from the Reverend Emerson's house, they ran headlong into a column of reinforcements led by Colonel Smith. (According to a family story told in later years, Jones watched the retreat from the doorway of his shed when a stray bullet tore into the wall beside him. The bullet hole is still visible.) But as usual with Colonel Smith, action was taken too late to be of value. In responding to Captain Laurie's call for help, "The Colonel ordered 2 or 3 companies," Lieutenant John Barker, of the King's Own, noted with disdain, "but put himself at their head, by which means stopped 'em from being (in) time enough, for being a very fat heavy man, he would not have reached the bridge in half an hour, tho' it was not a half mile to it." Smith's force, along with the bridge survivors, continued on as far as the Jones house and then turned back to Concord. While the Colonel spent the next two

The bullet hole in the
Elisha Jones house

A Colonial militiaman

hours pondering uncertainties, militia from all over Middlesex County and beyond were moving towards the area to help settle accounts.

Certain now that Concord had not been set afire, the provincials were content to hold what they had and await further developments. "When I crossed over the bridge," Corporal Barrett said, "there were two (British) dead and another almost dead. There were eight or ten that were wounded and a running and a hobbling about, looking back to see if we were after them."

The Americans carried their dead and wounded to the John Buttrick house. And with the bridge area quiet now, 21-year-old Ammi White, one of the Concord minutemen, stopped to examine the fallen redcoats. One of them, badly wounded, began to stir. Stricken by the emotion of the hour, and perhaps fearful that the redcoat might harm him, White suddenly raised his hatchet and burst the man's head open.

When Captain Parsons finally returned to the river with his companies, he was astonished to find planks torn up and dead and wounded infantrymen lying about. But when he and his soldiers saw the hacked remains of Ammi White's victim, they thought the provincials had resorted to scalping and quickly spread the word. As brutal as the act was, official accounts exaggerated the incident. Ensign Jeremy Lister, of the 10th Regiment, reported: ". . . There were 4 men of the 4th Company killed who were afterwards scalped, their eyes gouged, their noses and ears cut off; such barbarity exercised upon the Corps could scarcely be paralleled by the most uncivilized savages."

The Americans positioned near the bridge permitted Parsons and his shaken command to march into town without mishap. With the Barrett farm mission completed and other duties attended to, Colonel Smith put his force on the road back to Lexington at noon. It would have to be a spirited march. The safety of the Charles River was 17 miles away and the countryside was in a state of acute alarm.

So off they went, the wounded in carriages appropriated from townspeople, the light infantry again assigned the chore of sweeping the ridge north of the road. The withdrawal from Concord went well except for the fact that the men were tiring from the long march from Boston. At Meriam's Corner the ridge descends sharply to the road, and the light infantry, streaming down in a long scarlet line, fell in with the grenadiers and headed for a small bridge that spanned a stream of water at the Corner.

The Americans had been active as well. After moving from their positions at North Bridge, some of the provincials chose to march eastward behind Elisha Jones's house on a line parallel to that taken by the infantry to arrive at Meriam's Corner before the redcoats. One company from Reading was already in position, and additional companies had come to join the others. As Smith's men crossed the bridge, the adjoining roads and fields swarmed with armed provincials taking up positions behind stone walls, trees, houses, and outbuildings offering cover. The Reverend Ebenezer Foster, a private in a Reading company, noted: "The British marched down the hill with a very slow but steady step, without music or a word being spoken that could be heard. Silence reigned on both sides." Then, as the last of the redcoats passed over the bridge, shots were exchanged on both sides. A storm of shot ripped into the files of scarlet and white, knocking many from the ranks.

A British soldier

35

Lieutenant Barker reported that "before we had gone half a mile we were fired on from all sides, but mostly from the rear, where people had hid themselves in houses till we had passed, and then fired." Clearly the frontier manner of fighting did not appeal to the British who had long been accustomed to more organized battle tactics.

The Americans poured a driving fire on the rear and both flanks of the British column. "They were waylaid and a great many killed," Amos Barrett reported. "A great many lay dead and the road was bloody."

Smith's soldiers returned the fire, then continued on down the road to what they hoped would be safety. But, by now, hundreds of provincials were racing across the fields to take up new positions ahead. Troops from East Sudbury positioned themselves on Brooks Hill to fire down on the British.

The Bloody Angle

MOVING EASTWARD FROM THE JOB BROOKS HOUSE, THE ROADWAY WINDS SHARPLY to the north and curves through a wooded area. A large body of provincials had gathered here and, as the redcoats came into view, sent a thunderous volley into them. This bend in The Battle Road, called "The Bloody Angle," claimed eight British killed and many wounded. Three Americans lost their lives as well.

"In this way we marched . . . miles," Lieutenant Barker complained, "their numbers increasing from all parts while ours was reduced by deaths, wounds, and fatigue; and we were totally surrounded with such an incessant fire as it's impossible to conceive; our ammunition was likely near expended."

Colonel Smith, who had sent for reinforcements early that morning, now worried frantically whether or not they would arrive in time.

The Bloody Angle

The boulder on Nelson's farm which sheltered William Thorning

The light infantry moved off in broken lines to clear the nearby fields of sharpshooters, firing occasionally and often wildly until the scarlet column, its military propriety wearing thin, streamed past the doorway from which Mary Hartwell had witnessed the fine precision of the redcoats' march to Concord that morning. One of the men, wide-eyed with fear, paused long enough to fire a musket ball into the Hartwell garret. Another, as if in a blind rage, hurled his broken musket through one of the front windows.

Farther east on the north side of the road, lay two fields belonging to Josiah Nelson, the patriot who, sword gash in his head, had ridden to alert the Bedford company many hours before. The first field was scarred with grassy knolls and shallow furrows; the second studded with huge boulders. The Nelson family later told of William Thorning, a member of the Lincoln company, who entered the first field that morning, found a perfect point of observation and opened fire on the British. A sporadic return fire drove him back towards the woods where he suddenly saw a flanking party of light infantry about 100 feet away. Dropping into one of the furrows, Thorning lay still until the party had moved on. Then he ran into the second field and, sheltered behind a boulder, he fired several shots at the party, killing two of them. According to the story, both victims were buried on a knoll across the road. The boulder behind which Thorning sought shelter still lies in the field.

Meanwhile, Captain John Parker had rallied his Lexington company following the morning clash on the Green. Now with the British retreating eastward, Parker placed his militiamen on a hill east of Nelson's Bridge just inside the Lexington town line and waited for the redcoats. From their position,

The Bedford flag

Major John Pitcairn's pistols

Parker and his men could see the drifting smoke of musketry moving towards them. They made out the crouched figures of minutemen dashing across the rolling fields. Then the British came into view, firing in every direction. The left flank stumbled through Josiah Nelson's land on the north side of the road, while, to the south, a redcoat flanking party vaulted a stone wall lining Jacob Whittemore's field. Parker's men prepared to greet them.

At Fiske Hill the British began to panic. In an effort to restore order to his disorganized ranks, Major Pitcairn rode to the head of the column shouting orders. In the riot of gunfire and confusion, his horse suddenly threw him and ran off the road into the waiting arms of gleeful militiamen. With the animal went Pitcairn's prize pistols still in their saddle holsters.

Having no concealment whatever, the redcoats faced superior numbers and were totally exhausted. Added to their woes was a critical shortage of ammunition. But the provincials, with new companies arriving steadily, increased their strength by the hour. Soon all order in the scarlet ranks collapsed as the march turned into a rout. Ensign de Berniere, one of Smith's officers, commented: "When we arrived within a mile of Lexington our ammunition began to fail, and the light (infantry) companies were so fatigued with flanking they were scarce able to act, and a great number of wounded scarce able to get forward made a great confusion."

Colonel Smith had suffered a painful leg wound in the fighting. Realizing that his bulk made him a perfect target for ambitious provincial sharpshooters, he dismounted and limped along with his men.

Some of the stragglers from Smith's force broke into private homes in search of snipers or to pillage. One of them entered the Fiske house (on the south side of the road near the present Route 128), which was also used to care for wounded, and then went to the yard to refresh himself at the well. There he was discovered by James Hayward, an Acton minuteman. The redcoat snapped his musket up to cover Hayward and shouted: "You are a dead man!"

"And so are you!" the minuteman called back and each fired his weapon. Both fell to the ground, the soldier killed instantly, Hayward to die eight hours later. A monument just off the road marks the spot of the encounter.

As they neared Lexington, the British became a hapless lot. With morale dissipated and discipline a code of the hazy past, the men raced towards the center of town, each hoping desperately to escape with his life. At bayonet point, officers tried to regain control. "Upon this they began to form under a heavy fire," De Berniere reported, and in that fashion the King's troops staggered into Lexington proper and up to the Common where their morning's work had been undertaken with such grisly results. They were badly beaten now and every man knew it; at the Green where they had so eagerly begun their day, they could expect little sympathy. They were at the mercy of the provincials.

But on an elevation at the far end of town, the harassed soldiers saw a streak of scarlet that suddenly changed everything. For there on that elevation stood Smith's reinforcements under Brigadier General Hugh, Earl Percy, which numbered nearly a thousand regulars supported by fresh arms and two cannons. The battered light infantry and grenadiers ran to the safety of Percy's line.

Lieutenant Barker recognized the significance of Percy's appearance at that precise moment, for ". . . in all human probability must every man have

A militiaman's powder horn

41

been cut off if the Brigade had not fortunately come to their assistance; for when the Brigade joined us there were very few men had any ammunition left, and so fatigued that we could not keep flanking parties out, so that we must soon have laid down our arms or been picked off by the Rebels at their pleasure."

COLONEL SMITH'S MEN WERE SAFE, AT LEAST FOR THE MOMENT. THE SOLDIERS sank to the ground exhausted; wounded were treated at the Munroe Tavern. At the same time Americans were taking up positions behind stone walls and buildings. Groups of them could be seen dashing back and forth in the vicinity of the meeting house and at other points around the Common, rarely exposing themselves long enough for the redcoats to take aim. To discourage further attacks, Percy, now in full command, ordered his cannons up and sent off a few rounds to keep the provincials at a safe distance; at one point a six-pounder crashed through a wall of the meeting house. So other than for occasional sniping, the firing fell off. Percy then ordered the burning of three houses and three outbuildings from which further sniping could be expected.

On the American side, General William Heath arrived and tried to organize the various militia and minute units into a unified force, but to no avail.

Shortly after 3:00 that afternoon—about a half hour after the arrival of Smith's troops—Percy's command prepared to march out of Lexington. The Royal Welch Fusiliers were designated as rear guard for the 1800-man force, and Lieutenant Frederick Mackenzie, a member of that unit, recorded that the provincials resumed their fire from houses and other cover before the redcoats had marched a mile. "Several of the troops were killed and wounded in this way,

The Belfry Tower, Lexington

A Colonial pipe rack

and the soldiers were so enraged at suffering from an unseen enemy that they forced open many of the houses from which the fire proceeded, and put to death all those found in them."

Lieutenant Barker wrote in a similar vein: "We were now obliged to force almost every house in the road, for the Rebels had taken possession of them and galled us exceedingly; but they suffered for their temerity, for all that were found in the houses were put to death."

As Percy's column passed into the section of West Cambridge called Menotomy (now Arlington), the fighting became increasingly violent. Additional companies arrived to give renewed authority to American efforts; provincials out of ammunition pulled out of the fight while late arrivals took their places, swelling provincial ranks at this point to an estimated 1,900 men. Percy's flanking tactics were highly successful in this area, and a good many Yankees lost their lives as a result.

Jason Russell, almost sixty and a cripple, built a barricade of shingles in front of his house and prepared to defend himself and his property against the regulars, when a group of seven Danvers minutemen arrived seeking cover from an approaching party of flankers. The redcoats suddenly opened fire and Russell fell in the doorway; multiple bayonet thrusts ended his life. Then the flankers rushed inside and bayoneted to death all seven of the Danvers men. Eight other provincials were hiding in the cellar and, when discovered by the regulars, pointed their muskets up the stairs, daring the redcoats to enter. One did and was shot dead. (The Jason Russell house still stands near the corner of Jason Street and Massachusetts Avenue in Arlington.)

The Russell house marked the beginning of what was to be called "the bloodiest half mile of all the Battle Road." Some 20 Americans and even more British soldiers died on this stretch of country road that day.

"Even women had firelocks," a British eyewitness wrote a friend. "One was seen to fire a blunderbuss between her father and husband from their windows. There they three, with an infant child, soon suffered the fury of the day."

Hannah Adams lay in the bedroom of her home, having recently delivered a baby. Being "scarcely able to walk from my bed to the fire," she wrote of it, she made no attempt to flee when the British approached. And when two redcoats entered her room with bayonets fixed, she cried out: "For the Lord's sake do not kill me!"

His bayonet pointed at her breast, one soldier replied: "Damn you!"

Then the second soldier intervened, saying: "We will not hurt the woman if she will go out of the house, but we will surely burn it."

Placing a blanket about her, Mrs. Adams picked up her infant and struggled outside to the safety of the corn house. The soldiers set the house afire, but it was "happily extinguished" before much damage was done.

The redcoats fired more than a hundred bullets into the Cooper Tavern, and several soldiers entered the premises just after Benjamin and Rachel Cooper fled to the cellar. Inside, Jason Winship and his brother-in-law, Jabez Wyman, sat over their ale secure in the notion that because they were non-combatants no harm would come to them. Both were unarmed. Both were slain by British bayonets.

In spite of the successes of the flanking parties, the provincials kept up an

A Colonial pipe lighter

A pierced lantern

incessant fire on Percy's column, weakening their resolve along with the continuing ability to function effectively. "Our men had very few opportunities of getting good shots at the Rebels," Lieutenant Mackenzie wrote, "as they hardly ever fired but under cover of a stone wall, from behind a tree, or out of a house...." Such unorthodox battle tactics enraged a good many regulars, including Captain W. G. Evelyn, of the King's Own, who branded the Americans "the most absolute cowards on the face of the earth...."

By the time Percy's column crossed over the Menotomy River into Cambridge, it was showing signs of wear. The force had many wounded and everyone was tired. Percy took careful stock of his situation for darkness was not far off, and he was still some distance from the safety of Boston. He decided to abandon his plan to return to the city by way of the Charles River at the opposite end of Cambridge. Charlestown Neck was closer; and, in the waters there, British naval guns would offer ample protection against the provincials. As it turned out, Percy's decision was a good one. According to Barker, ". . . the Rebels, thinking we would endeavour to return by Cambridge, had broken down the bridge (over the Charles) and had a great number of men to line the road and to receive us there."

Finally, with darkness upon them, the British expedition dragged itself across Charlestown Neck and into the safety of the hilly terrain beyond where, as Ensign Lister noted, "the Rebels fire ceased they not having it in their power to pursue us any further in their skulking way behind hedges and walls...."

By nightfall some 4,000 provincials had spent some part of the 19th directing an almost constant fire on the regulars until Lord Percy guided them to the safety of Thomas Gage's troops in Boston. There the redcoats doctored their bodies and counted their casualties—73 dead, 174 wounded, and 26 missing. The Americans had suffered 49 killed (not all of them regular militia), 41 wounded, and 5 missing.

With it all, the British expedition to Concord had been a failure. The bulk of the military stores had not been destroyed and would soon be employed against them. The provincials had proven that they could give a good account of themselves. Even Lord Percy gave them their due:

"Whoever looks upon them as an irregular mob, will find himself much mistaken; they have men amongst them who know very well what they are about.... You may depend upon it, that as the rebels have now had time to prepare, they are determined to go through with it, nor will the insurrection here turn out so despicable as it is perhaps imagined at home."

Colonial resistance to the policies of the Crown had passed from the thunder of oratory to armies in the field. The American Revolution had begun....

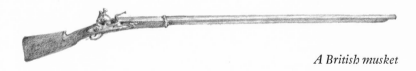

A British musket